CELEBRATING HOLIDAYS

Cinco de Mayo

by Rachel Grack

BELLWETHER MEDIA · MINNEAPOLIS, MN

Note to Librarians, Teachers, and Parents:

Blastoff! Readers are carefully developed by literacy experts and combine standards-based content with developmentally appropriate text.

Level 1 provides the most support through repetition of high-frequency words, light text, predictable sentence patterns, and strong visual support.

Level 2 offers early readers a bit more challenge through varied simple sentences, increased text load, and less repetition of high-frequency words.

Level 3 advances early-fluent readers toward fluency through increased text and concept load, less reliance on visuals, longer sentences, and more literary language.

Level 4 builds reading stamina by providing more text per page, increased use of punctuation, greater variation in sentence patterns, and increasingly challenging vocabulary.

Level 5 encourages children to move from "learning to read" to "reading to learn" by providing even more text, varied writing styles, and less familiar topics.

Whichever book is right for your reader, Blastoff! Readers are the perfect books to build confidence and encourage a love of reading that will last a lifetime!

This edition first published in 2018 by Bellwether Media, Inc.

No part of this publication may be reproduced in whole or in part without written permission of the publisher. For information regarding permission, write to Bellwether Media, Inc., Attention: Permissions Department, 5357 Penn Avenue South, Minneapolis, MN 55419.

Library of Congress Cataloging-in-Publication Data

Names: Koestler-Grack, Rachel A., 1973- author.
Title: Cinco de Mayo / by Rachel Grack.
Description: Minneapolis, MN : Bellwether Media, Inc., 2018 | Series:
  Blastoff! Readers: Celebrating Holidays | Includes bibliographical
  references and index. | Audience: Grades K-3. | Audience: Ages 5-8.
Identifiers: LCCN 2016052731 (print) | LCCN 2016054063 (ebook) | ISBN
  9781626176171 (hardcover : alk. paper) | ISBN 9781681033471 (ebook)
Subjects: LCSH: Cinco de Mayo (Mexican holiday)–History–Juvenile
  literature. | Mexico–Social life and customs–Juvenile literature. |
  Mexican Americans–Social life and customs–Juvenile literature. | Puebla,
  Battle of, Puebla de Zaragoza, Mexico, 1862–Juvenile literature.
Classification: LCC F1233 .K63 2017 (print) | LCC F1233 (ebook) | DDC
  394.262–dc23
LC record available at https://lccn.loc.gov/2016052731

Editor: Christina Leighton   Designer: Lois Stanfield

Printed in the United States of America, North Mankato, MN.

Table of Contents

Cinco de Mayo Is Here!

The **mariachi band** plays a **folk song**.

mariachi band

Dancers spin in colorful
dresses. People fill plates with
food. Cinco de Mayo is here!

What Is Cinco de Mayo?

site of the
Battle of Puebla

Cinco de Mayo honors the Battle of Puebla. The Mexican army won this battle against the French.

The holiday also celebrates Mexican **heritage**.

How Do You Say?

Word	Pronunciation
chalupas	chah-LOO-pahs
Cinco de Mayo	SEEN-koh dey MY-oh
fiesta	fee-ESS-tuh
mariachi	MAH-ree-AH-chee
mole poblano	MOH-ley poh-BLAH-noh
Puebla	PWEB-lah

Who Celebrates Cinco de Mayo?

People honor this day in Puebla, Mexico.

celebration in Puebla, Mexico

8

celebration in
New York City

Other parts of Mexico also throw
celebrations. Canada and the
United States celebrate, too.

Cinco de Mayo Beginnings

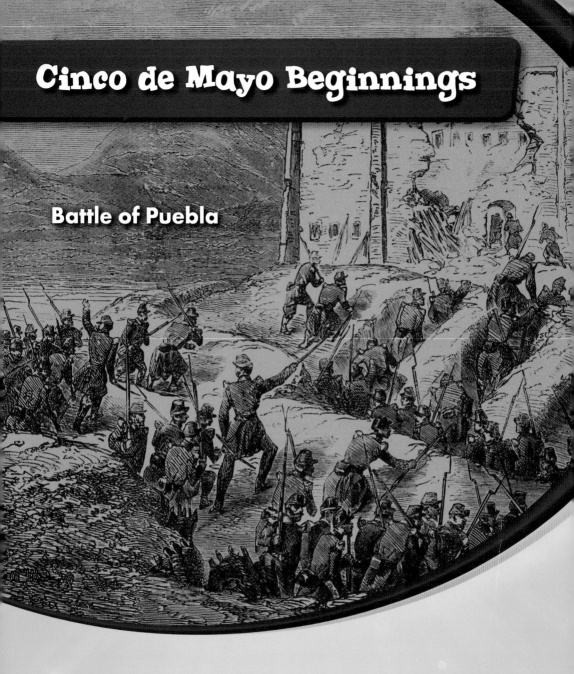

Battle of Puebla

In 1862, France attacked Puebla, Mexico.

Mexico had about 4,500 soldiers to fight the battle. France had about 6,000!

The Mexican army forced the French out. The win became a **symbol** of **independence**.

Battle of Puebla reenactment

It gave hope to the people
of Mexico.

The holiday falls on May 5
every year. The Battle of Puebla
took place on this date.

Cinco de Mayo is Spanish for "fifth of May."

Cinco de Mayo Traditions!

Many people have parties. They decorate with red, white, and green. These are the colors of the Mexican flag.

Battle of Puebla
reenactment

Some people **reenact** the battle.

People watch lively parades.
Floats are covered with bright
paper flowers. Violins and
trumpets play **traditional** music.

Make a Paper Flower

What You Need:
- 8 sheets of colored tissue paper
- scissors
- pipe cleaner
- ruler

What You Do:
1. Cut each piece of tissue paper to 7 inches by 11 inches.
2. Stack the sheets together.
3. Fold over one end of the short side to make a ¾-inch flap.
4. Continue folding the stacked tissue paper back and forth.
5. Cut off any extra tissue paper after you are done folding.
6. Round the ends with scissors.
7. Wrap the pipe cleaner around the center.
8. Spread one side of tissue paper open like a fan.
9. Carefully separate each layer of tissue paper.
10. Repeat steps 8 and 9 with the other side, and then fluff the tissue paper.

Families serve Mexican dishes. **Mole poblano** with chicken is a favorite meal.

mole poblano

chalupas

People also eat **chalupas** with salsa and meat. They enjoy **fiestas** on Cinco de Mayo!

Glossary

chalupas—thick, fried tortillas

fiestas—the Spanish word for parties

folk song—a song that was created by the people of an area or country

heritage—the history of a group of people

independence—freedom from being under control of someone or something

mariachi band—a group that plays Mexican music with trumpets, violins, and guitars

mole poblano—a rich and spicy chocolate sauce

reenact—to act out an event from the past

symbol—an object that stands for ideas or beliefs

traditional—the way past generations did something

To Learn More

AT THE LIBRARY

Rissman, Rebecca. *Cinco de Mayo*. Chicago, Ill.: Heinemann Library, 2011.

Sebra, Richard. *It's Cinco de Mayo!* Minneapolis, Minn.: Lerner Publications, 2017.

Smith, Maximilian. *The Story of Cinco de Mayo*. New York, N.Y.: Gareth Stevens Publishing, 2016.

ON THE WEB

Learning more about
Cinco de Mayo is as easy
as 1, 2, 3.

1. Go to www.factsurfer.com.

2. Enter "Cinco de Mayo" into the search box.

3. Click the "Surf" button and you will see a
   list of related web sites.

With factsurfer.com, finding more information
is just a click away.

Index